Panini and Other Great Grilled Sandwiches

Recipes for the
"Anytime, Anywhere" Meal

Dwayne Ridgaway

Contents

Introduction 7

Historical notes on the sandwich— how it was developed and when panini became an international item.

Making a Great Sandwich Every Time 8

Introduction

People love sandwiches. And why not? A sandwich can be an entire meal, ready to go anywhere. From picnics to poolside, from a quick weekend lunch to a daily routine, sandwiches are the easiest, most portable meal there is. As increasingly more cafés and delis pop up on city streets and corners across the country, the popularity of the sandwich is at an all-time high. The variety is just as numerous as the places to find them—from wraps, clubs, and pitas to panini and more.

The sandwich was actually created by accident in 1762. John Mantagu, the fourth Earl of Sandwich, was involved in a heated card game in which the stakes were high. He asked a servant to cook some meat and put it between two slices of bread so Montagu could eat his meal without geting his hands and cards dirty!

Sandwich history is a melting pot of cultural influence. Bread is found in some form or another in just about every culture, as are meat, vegetables, and cheese. Although it doesn't appear that one culture contributed more to sandwich history than another, it's clear by the number of Italian cold cuts available at any deli counter that Italy played a part in sandwich history. Panini, the latest trend in sandwich making, is also Italian for sandwich. In this country, Americans define panini as a grilled or pressed sandwich served warm, while an authentic Italian panini can be served hot or cold. In this book, I use the term *panini* to refer to grilled sandwiches.

While the ingredients of a panini can vary widely, the technique used to make one is one and the same. Start by piling a variety of succulent ingredients between two moist pieces of bread, oil or butter them, then press them between two hot grill plates, which toast the outside and melt the ingredients on the inside. Many other ingredients can also be prepared on the same grill. Meats and fish as well as vegetables can be cooked with the panini grill open (grilling with the bottom plate only) or closed to quickly grill with both the top and bottom plates.

This book will cover much more than paninis, however. I plan to take you on a culinary journey that will not only please your palate but also offer exciting sandwich accompaniments, condiments, and serving suggestions.

I will also teach you some basics behind selecting bread, explore interesting and new sandwich ingredients, and introduce you to techniques for easy sandwich building. With recipes for cold, hot, vegetarian, and salad sandwiches, there's something for everyone in this book. My recipes range from traditional to unique, and from simple to more involved, so beginner and experienced home cooks alike will find a sandwich to suit their skills and tastes.

Making a Great Sandwich Every Time

[Bread]

Bread, in one form or another, is essential to making a great sandwich, whether it's sliced, flattened, wrapped, stuffed, or folded. Bread, as with all the ingredients, is a very personal choice. The qualities of breads range from firm, dense, airy, or hard to soft, thick, thin, white, wheat, sourdough, herbed, and more.

The basic rules to remember are as follows: Is the bread strong enough to hold the ingredients together? Is the bread dense enough to hold a sauce or oil? Is the bread large enough to accommodate the ingredients? Is the bread thin or thick enough, depending on the number of fillings? All of these are very basic points, but ones that can determine whether or not your sandwich is successful.

The flavor of the bread is as important as its size and shape. The bread should complement the inner ingredients. For example, a cinnamon raisin bread doesn't pair well with grilled tuna and wasabi mayonnaise, just as pumpernickle bread is probably too intense for everyday ham and cheese. When selecting the bread, keep in mind that all the flavors will have to work together.

[Meat]

If you've visited your local deli counter recently, you're probably well aware of the wide variety of cold cuts available, not to mention other choices such as barbecued pork, grilled chicken, or cooked seafood. Meat, like bread, is a personal choice that really relies on the other ingredients around it to make the whole sandwich. When building a sandwich, keep in mind the flavor and the texture of the meat you select, as well the cooking temperature (if any) and preparation methods.

If you are making sandwiches ahead of time, food safety is paramount. Make sure all sandwiches made with meat and cold cuts are kept as cold as possible; meat can spoil under adverse temperatures, so I recommend using ice or cold packs to keep the sandwiches fresh and safe.

When traveling, I recommend packing all your sandwich ingredients separately and building the sandwich once you reach your destination, but in some cases, this won't be practical. If you pack everything separately, be sure to bring along condiments and utensils, and keep all ingredients well chilled in airtight containers.

[A note about grilling chicken]

The recipes in this book call for you to grill chicken on high heat until cooked through, about 7 minutes. However, the cooking time will vary according to the thickness of the chicken and the temperature of the grill. If in doubt, the internal temperature of the cooked chicken should reach at least 165°F (75°C).

[Vegetables]

The main question relating to vegetables is whether they are used raw or cooked. Both types work fine for sandwich making, but, as with all ingredients, make sure they complement each other. The cut of the vegetable is also important. Slicing certain vegetables too thick will make the sandwich hard to eat, while if you slice them too thin, the flavors will be lost. If using grilled vegetables, I recommend a ¼-inch (6 mm) thick slice, so the vegetables, don't cook too fast and/or fall apart. Certain vegetables such as lettuce, should always be used raw, but spinach works fine served raw or cooked.

The following ingredients appear in several recipes and are excellent options for many of your own recipes.

Roasted Peppers

One pepper makes about ½ cup (120 g) of sliced roasted pepper

Any bell pepper variety— red, yellow, orange, green, or purple—works well for roasting.

The easiest way to roast peppers is by using a gas grill. Preheat the grill to high. Coat the peppers evenly with olive oil and place on the grill. Cook the peppers until the skin is charred black, turning them periodically to ensure even roasting. If you do not have a gas grill, I recommend using the broiler in your oven. Preheat the broiler, then place the oiled

peppers in a shallow roasting pan under the broiler on the middle rack of the oven. Broil until skin is black, turning them occasionally to ensure even roasting.

Once the skin is charred black, transfer the peppers to a paper or plastic bag. Seal the bag and set aside for 5 minutes. Remove peppers from the bag and remove blackened skin, slice, and remove seeds. Use roasted peppers immediately, or refrigerate for up to 5 days.

Roasted Garlic

Roasting garlic is a technique that concentrates the flavors of raw garlic into an intense, robust, earthy flavor and aroma. Like truffle oil, the flavor and smell of roasted garlic is distinctive and easily recognizable. If you don't like the taste of raw garlic, I encourage you to try this technique, as roasted garlic is unique and enjoyable.

Makes about ½ cup (120 g)

4 heads fresh garlic, stem ends removed to ½" (1.25 cm)

2 tablespoons (30 ml) olive oil

Salt

Coarse ground black pepper

Preheat the oven to 375°F (190°C). Place the garlic, cut ends up, in an oven-safe pan or dish. Drizzle each head with olive oil and season with salt and pepper. Place in oven and roast for 30 to 45 minutes or until garlic is a rich brown, caramelized color and the cloves are easily pierced with the sharp tip of a knife. Remove from oven and let cool. If not using immediately, store refrigerated in an airtight container for up to one week. If using immediately, remove the roasted cloves by pinching the ends of each clove to force the garlic from the skin.

[Cheese]

Cheese is my favorite part of a sandwich. It's a bit more complicated than some other ingredients, however, because of the differences from one variety to another. When selecting cheese, keep in mind its texture, melting ability, spreadability, and flavor intensity. Melting ability is obviously critical if you are making a hot sandwich. Some varieties of cheese just don't melt well and others can be too runny. Swiss cheese, for example, is used in a Reuben because the flavor is strong enough to pair well with the robust flavors of rye bread, sauerkraut, and corned beef, while its melting ability makes it soft but not runny. Spreading cheeses—such as cream cheese, Boursin, and goat cheese— also make great additions to a sandwich. These three types of cheese offer intense flavors with a subtle texture that lend themselves well to certain applications, but goat cheese and Boursin do not melt well. My advice? Know who you are serving, as many cheeses require an acquired taste.

[Spreads and Condiments]

Think of spreads and condiments as the glue that holds the sandwich together. There are literally hundreds of packaged condiments and spreads available for use on sandwiches, but I believe homemade is still the best. Don't be afraid to experiment. As with any sandwich ingredient, the main thing to keep in mind is that all the elements work well together.

[Sandwich Construction]

The layers of a sandwich speak volumes about the maker and the eater. It's said there's even a secret society that believes in the art of interpreting a sandwich, its contents, and how they relate to the eater or the builder. While I can't teach you the psychology of the sandwich, I will stress that the order in which you assemble a sandwich can be crucial to the enjoyment. If your tomatoes slip out, it's a big mess. Cheese placed in the middle of a sandwich won't melt, and lettuce belongs around everything else. While there is no real science behind the construction of a sandwich, after making hundreds for this book, here's my definition of the right order:

1. Bread
2. Condiment
3. Cheese—if hot
4. Lettuce—if cold
5. Cheese—if cold
6. Tomato or other vegetable
7. Meat
8. Cheese again—if cold
9. Lettuce again—if cold
10. Cheese again—if hot
11. Condiment
12. Bread

[Making the Sandwiches]

Each of the recipes in this book instructs you on how to make one sandwich using the ingredients called for in the recipe. After completing one sandwich, the recipe will instruct you to repeat the process to assemble the remaining sandwiches. Take care to split the ingredients evenly among all the sandwiches.

The word *panini* is actually the Italian term for sandwich. Because of the popularity of the Italian technique of grilling or pressing a sandwich to heat and toast it, panini has been adapted to refer specifically to this style of hot sandwich. Throughout this book, I refer to panini as sandwiches that are pressed or grilled. Whether you use a panini grill or a stovetop skillet, the technique is simple. Build your sandwich with the appropriate ingredients, spread oil or butter on the outside of both sides of the bread, and grill or toast.

1 lb (455 g) honey-baked deli ham, sliced thin

8 slices Swiss cheese

6 ounces (170 g) baby spinach

Whole Grain Molasses Mustard (see page 112)

Shaved-Apple Salad (recipe follows)

Butter, room temperature

8 slices pumpernickel bread

FOR SHAVED-APPLE SALAD:

Makes about 2 cups (475 ml)

½ cup (112 g) mayonnaise

1 tablespoon (14 g) sour cream

1 tablespoon (20 g) honey

1 tablespoon (15 ml) cider vinegar

1 teaspoon (3 g) brown sugar

1 cup (90 g) red cabbage, thinly sliced

½ red onion, thinly sliced

1 Granny Smith apple, peeled, cored, and grated on the coarse grate of a box grater, then tossed with the juice of 1 lemon

1 tablespoon (6 g) fresh chopped mint

Salt

Coarse ground black pepper

Preheat the panini grill to medium. Lay pumpernickel bread on a clean, flat, and dry work surface. Spread one slice of bread with molasses mustard, then layer with ham, spinach, apple salad, and two slices Swiss cheese. Spread molasses mustard on second bread slice and top sandwich. Butter both sides of sandwich and grill for about 7 minutes or until browned and crisp and cheese is melted. (Sandwich may also be individually wrapped in aluminum foil and baked at 400°F [200°C] for about 20 minutes.) Repeat process with remaining ingredients to make additional sandwiches. Remove from heat, slice, and serve warm.

[For shaved-apple salad]
Combine mayonnaise, sour cream, honey, cider vinegar, and brown sugar in medium bowl and stir. Add cabbage, onion, apple, and mint and toss until well incorporated, then season with salt and pepper. Set aside until ready for assembly.

[Makes 4 sandwiches]

Honey-Baked Ham Panini with Shaved-Apple Salad

The combination of apples and baked or roasted ham is phenomenal at any time of year, but it is especially welcome in autumn. A traditional coleslaw recipe is given a crisp, tangy twist with the addition of apples, which complement the honey-baked ham perfectly.

Southwestern
Spicy Beef Panini
with Black Bean Pesto

The flavors that the Southwest provides are brilliant. This is a classic steak and cheese gone south of the border.

2 tablespoons (30 ml) olive oil

1 pound (455 g) shaved beef sirloin

1 small red onion, thinly sliced

1 tablespoon (10 g) chopped fresh garlic

Parsley, chopped (to taste)

1½ tablespoons (20 ml) chili-garlic sauce*

8 slices of ciabatta bread or favorite hearty sandwich bread

1 roasted red pepper, thinly sliced (see recipe, page 28)

6 ounces (170 g) Monterey Jack cheese, shredded

*Chili-garlic sauce can be found in Asian markets or the Asian section of your local grocery store.

BLACK BEAN PESTO:

2 tablespoons (20 g) minced garlic

2 Serrano chilies, seeded and minced

1 (14-ounce [400 g]) can black beans, rinsed and drained

1 tablespoon (15 ml) rice vinegar

2 tablespoons (30 ml) olive oil

2 tablespoons (4 g) chopped fresh cilantro

1 green onion, chopped

1 tablespoon (7 g) ground cumin

3 drops chipotle pepper sauce (Tabasco brand is good quality)

Heat olive oil in a medium sauté pan over medium-high heat. Sauté beef, red onion, and garlic for about 3 minutes. Add chili-garlic sauce and continue cooking for an additional 4 minutes, until beef is cooked through. Add chopped parsley and season with salt and pepper. Remove from heat, set aide.

Preheat panini grill. Working on a flat, clean, and dry surface, lay out 4 slices of bread. Spread each slice with black bean pesto, top with beef mixture, roasted red pepper, and shredded Monterey Jack cheese; finish with remaining slice of bread. Spread butter evenly over top slices. Place sandwich on grilling surface, butter side down, butter additional sides and cook for 10 minutes until browned and crisp. Remove from heat, let rest for 3 minutes, then slice in half and serve.

[For the black bean pesto]
Working in the bowl of a food processor fitted with the blade attachment, add all the ingredients. Process until ingredients are chopped and well combined. Remove and set aside.

2 cups (100 g) packed fresh basil leaves, blanched, plus 24 additional leaves (not blanched)

1 cup (235 ml) extra-virgin olive oil

Salt and coarse ground black pepper

1 loaf ciabatta bread or panini bread, sliced about ½-inch (1 cm) thick

2 cloves roasted garlic (see recipe, page 29)

1 pound (455 g) buffalo mozzarella cheese, cut into 18 slices

Butter at room temperature

[Makes 6 sandwiches]

Italian Grilled Cheese Panini with Basil Oil

Italians love their tomatoes and mozzarella. What better a way to enjoy them than between two crisp, toasted pieces of bread with basil oil? Any good-quality melting cheese can be used in this panini, but the rich, velvety texture of fresh mozzarella truly celebrates the Italian flavor. Use garden-fresh basil for the basil oil to add zip to the flavors.

In the bowl of a food processor fitted with the blade attachment, place the blanched basil and olive oil. Blend on high until all the basil is chopped and oil appears bright green. Strain oil through a fine sieve or cheesecloth into a bowl, season with salt and black pepper, and set aside.

Preheat panini grill. Working on a flat, clean, and dry work surface, lay out 6 slices of bread. Spread roasted garlic on each slice of bread. Divide mozzarella cheese slices among the 6 slices of bread, layering evenly. Top with sliced tomato and reserved basil leaves. Drizzle tomatoes with basil oil. Top with remaining 6 slices of bread.

Spread butter on top pieces, coating bread evenly. Place sandwiches on grilling surface, butter side down, then butter additional side, lower lid and and cook for 10 minutes until browned and crisp. Remove from heat, let rest for 3 minutes, then slice in half and serve.

3 tablespoons (45 ml) vegetable oil

⅓ cup (40 g) minced celery

4 green onions, minced

½ cup (58 g) dried bread crumbs

1 lb (455 g) lump crab meat, picked over for any shell

1 egg

2 tablespoons (8 g) minced parsley

¼ cup (15 g) fresh chopped cilantro

1 red bell pepper, diced

⅓ cup (75 g) mayonnaise

1 cup (240 ml) Grilled Onion Relish (see recipe, page 110)

½ cup (120 ml) Spicy Tartar Sauce (see recipe, page 110)

4 onion sandwich rolls, grilled in a panini grill

Heat 3 tablespoons (45 ml) vegetable oil in a sauté pan. Add celery, green onion, and red pepper, then sauté until tender, about 3 minutes. Add bread crumbs and brown for one minute. Remove from heat and transfer to mixing bowl, and let cool for 10 minutes. Add crab, egg, parsley, cilantro, and mayonnaise, stir to combine, then season with salt and pepper. Form crab mixture into 4-inch (10 cm) balls, then flatten into a disk shape. (The crab cakes should fit comfortably on the onion roll.)

Preheat oven to 400°F (200°C) and panini grill to medium heat. Cook crab cakes until well done, about 7 minutes per side. Repeat the process to cook all the crab cakes. Transfer cakes to a sheet pan and bake in oven for 10 minutes. Remove from oven and place crab cake on bottom half of onion roll, then top with generous amount of tartar sauce, onion relish, and top half of roll. Repeat process with remaining ingredients to make additional sandwiches. Serve.

[Makes 4 sandwiches]

Crab Cake Panini with Grilled Onion Relish and Spicy Tartar Sauce

Crab cakes, while good on their own, can take on a new life as a panini. This one is no exception; the burst of flavor from the onion relish is very satisfying. If you prefer a more health-conscious version, serve the crab cake on a bed of greens without the bread.

1 italian eggplant, sliced horizontally into ½" (1.3 cm)-thick slices

1 small zucchini, sliced horizontally into ½" (1.3 cm)-thick slices

1 red pepper, roasted and sliced (see recipe, page 28)

1 red onion, sliced into ½" (1.3 cm)-thick slices

2 portobello mushroom caps, stems trimmed

½ cup (120 ml) olive oil, plus extra for brushing

Salt

Coarse ground black pepper

8 slices crusty ciabatta or other sandwich bread

4 pieces red leaf lettuce

⅓ cup (75 ml) Herbed Feta Spread (see recipe, page 113)

Balsamic vinegar

Preheat panini grill to medium-high. Brush eggplant, zucchini, onion slices, and portobello mushrooms evenly with olive oil, then season with salt and pepper. Place on hot grill and leaving the grill open, cook until browned and tender, about 4 minutes per side for eggplant and zucchini, 6 minutes per side for the onion, and 8 minutes per side for the mushrooms. Remove from grill and let cool. Peel the purple skin from the eggplant slices. Cut the onion rings in half.

Reduce panini grill to medium. Lay out bread, spread bottom with herbed feta spread, and layer with eggplant, lettuce, zucchini, onion, mushroom, and red pepper. Spread second bread slice with feta spread and place on top of sandwich, feta side down. Brush both sides of sandwich evenly and generously with olive oil, and grill, about 10 minutes.

Repeat process with remaining ingredients to make additional sandwiches. Slice and serve warm.

[Makes 4 sandwiches]

Grilled Vegetable Panini with Herbed Feta Spread

Grilling vegetables results in very concentrated, robust flavors that work well in a sandwich.

4 tablespoons (55 g) butter

2 tablespoons (30 ml) olive oil, plus additional for brushing

2 small, sweet yellow onions, sliced thin

1 lb (455 g) assorted wild mushrooms, sliced

1 teaspoon (5 g) sugar

1 tablespoon (3 g) lemon thyme

Salt

Coarse ground black pepper

6 ounces (170 g) fontina cheese, sliced

4 ounces (115 g) fresh buffalo mozzarella cheese, sliced

12 slices crusty ciabatta bread

Melt butter and olive oil in a large skillet over medium-high heat. Sauté onions, stirring occasionally. When the onions begin to wilt, reduce the heat to medium and add the mushrooms and sugar. Toss to combine, then continue to sauté, stirring occasionally until mixture becomes a dark caramel color, about 10 minutes. (Reduce heat if the onions and mushrooms become crisp; they should remain tender.) Add lemon thyme and toss to combine, then remove from heat and set aside.

Preheat panini grill to medium. Place bread on a flat, clean, and dry work surface, then layer with fontina and mozzarella cheeses. Add second slice of bread, brush top with olive oil, and place, oiled side down, on grilling surface. Brush top with olive oil and grill until cheese is melted and bread is browned and crisp, about 10 minutes. Repeat process with remaining ingredients to make additional sandwiches.

Keep the first batch warm in a 200°F (90°C) oven. Pull sandwiches apart and insert onion/mushroom mixture, then close, slice, and serve warm.

[Makes 6 sandwiches]

Fontina Panini **with Caramelized Onion and Mushroom Relish**

Fontina is a great melting cheese with an intense, almost earthy flavor that lends itself nicely to the flavors of assorted wild mushrooms. The choice of mushrooms is up to you, but I recommend shitake, oyster, and porcini.

Grilled Tuna Panini with Wasabi Ginger Mayonnaise

This delicious summer sandwich pairs grilled tuna steaks with wasabi mayonnaise. Tuna steaks on the grill are a special indulgence. The sauce or marinade for tuna steaks needs only to be subtle to enhance the flavor. Tuna paired with wasabi mayonnaise ensures a perfect summer sandwich.

Combine mayonnaise, wasabi paste, ginger, and lemon juice in a mixing bowl, stir to combine, and refrigerate for at least 30 minutes. Preheat panini grill to high. Combine olive oil, pepper, salt, and lemongrass in a small mixing bowl. Brush each tuna steak on both sides with the olive oil mixture. Place on hot grill and cook until browned but still pink in the middle, about 10 minutes. Butter both sides of roll and grill until toasted on both sides, about 5 minutes. Lay out bottom roll and layer with lettuce, cucumber, wasabi mayonnaise, and tuna steak. Add remaining mayonnaise and top of roll. Repeat process with remaining ingredients to make additional sandwiches. Serve.

4 (¹⁄₄-lb [115 g]) tuna steaks	4 portuguese english muffins
¹⁄₄ cup (60 ml) extra-virgin olive oil	¹⁄₄ cup (112 g) prepared mayonnaise
1 teaspoon (2 g) coarse ground black pepper	1 tablespoon (15 g) wasabi paste
¹⁄₂ teaspoon (3 g) kosher salt	1 teaspoon (3 g) freshly grated ginger
¹⁄₂ teaspoon (.5 g) dried lemongrass (optional)	¹⁄₂ teaspoon (2.5 ml) lemon juice
	4 leaves Bibb lettuce
	1 english cucumber, thinly sliced

4 (8-ounce [225 g])
boneless, skinless chicken breasts

olive oil

1 tablespoon (6 g) coarse
ground black pepper

2 tablespoons (20 g)
chopped fresh garlic

2 medium red peppers

$\frac{1}{2}$ lb (225 g) sharp
provolone cheese, thinly sliced

8 ounces (225 g)
mozzarella cheese, thinly sliced

12 leaves fresh basil

8 ounces (225 g) sliced pepperoni

6 ciabatta rolls

$\frac{1}{4}$ cup (60 ml) Roasted
Garlic Aioli (see recipe, page 111)

Preheat panini grill to high. Combine chicken breasts with 4 tablespoons (60 ml) olive oil, pepper, and garlic. On a platter, rub each red pepper generously with olive oil. Place chicken and red peppers on grill. Grill chicken 7 minutes, until browned and cooked through (the internal temperature should reach 165°F [75°C]). Transfer chicken to a cutting board and let cool. When cool enough to handle, cut into thin strips and set aside.

Grill red peppers, charring the skin black all over, about 20 minutes total. Transfer to a paper bag and seal, then let sit for about 5 minutes. Remove peppers from bag and peel away charred skin, leaving bright red flesh. Remove stem, seeds, and pulp, then cut into thick strips and set aside.

Brush inside of roll with olive oil, place on grill, oiled side down, and toast until golden brown. Transfer to plate. Lay out bottom half of roll, toasted side up, and spread with garlic aioli. Top with provolone, basil, pepperoni, chicken, red pepper, mozzarella, and finally top of roll, toasted side down. Wrap sandwich in aluminum foil. Reduce heat on grill to low. Place sandwich on grill and cook for 7 minutes, until cheese is melted. Repeat process with remaining ingredients to make additional sandwiches. Remove from foil, slice in half, and serve.

[Makes 6 sandwiches]

Chicken Soprano Panini

I'm sure Tony Soprano would enjoy this sandwich, which is so named for the Italian meats and cheeses found within.

Pickled Pastrami Panini

The traditional pastrami on rye sandwich is one of my favorites, and there is no substitution for good-quality pastrami. Here, pickles, mustard, and pastrami are united on this grilled panini, in a mouth-watering tribute to a classic.

8 slices farmhouse loaf or multigrain bread

⅓ cup (75 ml) Dijon mustard

1 lb (455 g) pastrami, hickory smoked or peppered, thinly sliced

2 kosher-style pickles, cut lengthwise into thin slices

¼ lb (115 g) Swiss cheese

olive oil for brushing

Preheat panini grill to medium. Place bread on a clean, flat, and dry work surface and spread with Dijon mustard. Top with 1 slice Swiss cheese, pastrami, pickles, remaining slice of Swiss cheese, and top half of bread. Brush top with olive oil, then place sandwich on panini grill, oiled side down, and brush top with olive oil. Grill until bread is browned and crisp and cheese is melted, about 10 minutes if using panini grill or 7 minutes per side if using skillet. Repeat process with remaining ingredients to make additional sandwiches. Remove from grill, slice, and serve.

Paris Texas Panini

I think Texas is the only place you can visit Paris, London, and Rome and never leave the United States. This panini, however, brings together an assortment of international flavors. When buying hot sauce, I recommend a brand called Chilulah.

1 french baguette

3 (6-ounce [170 g]) boneless, skinless chicken breasts

1 (6-ounce [170 g]) can green enchilada sauce

1 teaspoon (5 ml) hot sauce

1 teaspoon (2 g) cumin

¼ teaspoon (.3 g) dried oregano

1 teaspoon (2 g) coarse ground black pepper

3 tablespoons (30 g) chopped fresh garlic

8 ounces (225 g) Monterey Jack cheese, sliced

6 ounces (170 g) monchego cheese, sliced

4 poblano peppers

1 large white onion, thinly sliced

Olive oil

Preheat grill to high. Combine enchilada sauce, hot sauce, cumin, oregano, pepper, and garlic in a large bowl, and stir to combine. Add chicken, toss to coat, then cover and refrigerate for at least 30 minutes. Rub poblano peppers and onions with olive oil and place on hot grill. Grill onions about 4 minutes on each side until browned. Remove and set aside. Grill peppers, charring all sides until skin is black and blistered, about 15 minutes. Transfer to a paper bag and seal, then let sit for about 5 minutes. Remove peppers from bag and peel away charred skin. Remove stem, seeds, and pulp, then set aside.

Remove chicken from refrigerator and grill for about 7 minutes, until cooked through and browned (the internal temperature should reach 165°F [75°C]). Remove from grill and set aside.

Cut baguette into four equal pieces, then slice each piece horizontally, taking care not to cut all the way through. Fold bread open and with inside facing up, press down to flatten. Turn bread to work with what would be the outside of the loaf. On bottom half of bread, layer monchego and Monterey Jack cheeses. Close bread inside out. Spread butter on top and bottom and grill until browned and cheese is melted through, about 5 minutes. Meanwhile, slice chicken in thin strips with the grain and set aside. Remove sandwiches from grill. Open up and layer with poblano peppers, onion, and chicken. Close sandwich and slice in half. Repeat process with remaining ingredients to make additional sandwiches. Serve warm.

Bacon Cheddar Panini on Raisin Bread

I really enjoy the savory flavor of pepper-smoked bacon combined with the sweetness of raisins. This sandwich makes a great hurry-up-and-go breakfast, combining the sweet and savory with melted cheddar cheese. The kids will love this one on the way to school.

12 slices thick, peppered or smoked bacon, cooked

6 ounces (170 g) sharp white cheddar cheese, sliced

12 slices raisin bread

3 tablespoons (45 g) butter, room temperature

Preheat panini grill. Place raisin bread on flat, clean, and dry work surface. Layer with cheddar cheese, bacon, more cheddar cheese, and second bread slice. Butter both sides of sandwich and grill until browned and crisp and cheese is melted, about 10 minutes. Repeat process with remaining ingredients to make additional sandwiches. Serve.

12 slices rye bread

4 tablespoons (60 g)
butter, softened

1 cup (225 g) prepared
russian dressing

2 tablespoons (30 g)
german-style mustard

1½ lbs (680 g) deli pastrami
or corned beef, thinly sliced

½ lb (225 g)
Gruyere cheese, sliced

1 cup (225 g) sauerkraut

[Makes 6 sandwiches]

Irish Reuben Panini

It may be a culture clash to call a
Reuben a panini, but this multicultural
sandwich sure is good.

Preheat panini grill to medium-high heat. Preheat oven to 375°F (190°C). Working on a clean, flat, and dry surface, lay out rye bread. Spread with russian dressing, then layer Gruyere cheese, pastrami, sauerkraut, and more pastrami, Gruyere cheese, and russian dressing. Top with a second slice of bread. Butter both sides of bread and cook until one side is browned, about 5 minutes. Flip sandwich over and place on a hot baking sheet in oven to melt cheese. Repeat process with remaining ingredients to make additional sandwiches. Remove from oven, slice, and serve.

Pressed Cubano Chicken Sandwich

A staple of the Cuban population of Tampa and Miami, Florida, the Cubano is traditionally served on Cuban bread with roast pork and ham. My version combines roasted chicken with bacon on a sweet Hawaiian or Portuguese roll. If you are lucky enough to live in an area in which Cuban bread is available, then you may stick to the classic, but don't be afraid to experiment with a new twist.

1 teaspoon (5 ml) olive oil

1 garlic clove, minced

4 portuguese sweet rolls or hawaiian rolls, sliced in half horizontally

3 tablespoons (45 g) yellow mustard

2 tablespoons (32 g) sweet pickle relish

8 slices ($\frac{1}{2}$ ounce [15 g] each) Swiss cheese

8 slices bacon, cooked

$\frac{1}{4}$ cup (5 g) whole cilantro leaves

6 ounces (170 g) oven-roasted ham, thinly sliced

6 ounces (170 g) roasted chicken breast, thinly sliced

Preheat panini grill to medium heat. Combine oil and garlic in small bowl and set aside. Combine mustard and sweet relish in second bowl. Spread bottom half of each roll evenly with mustard/relish mixture. Layer with Swiss cheese, bacon, cilantro leaves, ham, chicken, and top half of roll. Grill until bread is toasted and cheese is melted, about 10 minutes. Remove from grill and let sit for 5 minutes. Repeat process with remaining ingredients to make additional sandwiches. Cut each in half and served stacked with skewered banana peppers.

Lemon Thyme–Roasted Chicken Panini with Havarti and Oven-Dried Tomatoes

Lemon thyme is an herb that is not always readily available in the grocery stores, but it adds tremendous flavor to many dishes. I recommend buying lemon thyme seeds or seedlings in late spring, when the garden shops stock up with herbs for the garden. Even potted, it will grow quickly and heartily and will then be available all summer long for cooking.

3 (6-ounce [170 g]) boneless, skinless chicken breasts

6 stems lemon thyme

1 lemon, sliced in half lengthwise and then cut into thin slices

6 Roma tomatoes

olive oil

coarse ground black pepper

Kosher salt

1 large parisian loaf, ends removed, cut in quarters

4 tablespoons (60 g) butter, room temperature

6 ounces (170 g) creamy Havarti cheese, sliced

½ cup (120 ml) ricotta cheese

2 ounces (60 g) frisée or other leafy greens

4 stems fresh italian flat-leaf parsley

Preheat oven to 400°F (200°C). Coat an ovenproof skillet (preferably cast iron) with non-stick cooking spray. Clean and butterfly chicken breasts horizontally. Fold each chicken breast open, top with two stems of lemon thyme and 3 slices of lemon, sprinkle with kosher salt and pepper, and close. Repeat with remaining chicken breasts. Place chicken breasts in skillet and drizzle with olive oil. Roast in oven until cooked through and browned on top, about 45 minutes. Remove and let cool, then remove thyme stems and lemon slices. Slice chicken into thin strips, cutting with the grain, and set aside.

Remove stem end of tomatoes. Line a sheet pan with parchment paper and coat with nonstick cooking spray. Cut tomatoes into ¼-inch (0.6 cm)-thick slices from top to bottom. Place on parchment paper and sprinkle with salt and pepper. Roast in 400°F (200°C) oven until shriveled and partially dried, about 45 minutes. Remove and set aside to cool.

Preheat panini grill. Slice loaves in half horizontally, taking care not to cut all the way through. Gently fold loaves open with both hands. Lay on flat surface with the inside of the bread facing up, then press firmly down on the loaf to flatten it. Layer bottom half with havarti and ricotta cheeses. Close bread, butter one side, and place on grill, buttered side down. Butter remaining side, then grill until browned and cheese is melted, about 5 minutes.

Transfer sandwiches to a plate, open and insert oven-dried tomatoes, sliced chicken, and greens. Repeat process with remaining ingredients to make additional sandwiches. Close sandwich, cut in half, and serve.

3 tablespoons (45 g)
unsalted butter

¼ cup (60 ml) extra-virgin olive
oil, plus 3 tablespoons (45 ml)

2 (10-ounce [284 g]) packages
bella or crimini mushrooms,
cleaned and cut in quarters

1 cup (100 g) sliced
shitake mushrooms

8 cloves garlic, minced and
then divided

1 teaspoon (1 g) fresh
chopped thyme

1 tablespoon (15 ml)
balsamic vinegar

½ teaspoon (1 g) coarse ground
black pepper

½ teaspoon (3 g) kosher salt

1 ciabatta loaf, sliced into ½"
(1.3 cm)-thick slices

½ cup (75 g)
mascarpone cheese

8 ounces (225 g) fontina
cheese, thinly sliced

Preheat oven broiler. In a large skillet over medium-high heat, melt the butter and add 3 tablespoons (45 ml) olive oil. When hot, add 4 cloves minced garlic and bella and shitake mushrooms. Saute for 3 minutes, then add thyme, pepper, salt, and balsamic vinegar and cook for 3 additional minutes or until mushrooms are tender but not soft. Remove from heat and set aside.

Combine remaining minced garlic with remaining olive oil in a small bowl. Brush one side of 8 slices of bread with olive oil/garlic mixture, lay on sheet pan and toast under broiler on middle rack until browned, about 3 minutes. Remove, spread with mascarpone, and top with fontina. Place under broiler on middle rack until cheese is melted, about 3 minutes. Remove, top with mushroom mixture, and serve warm.

[Makes 6 sandwiches]

Open-Faced Fontina Melt

In my mind, the concept of an open-faced sandwich is really a contradiction in terms. Regardless, this recipe is so tasty that I had to share it. For hors d'oeuvres, prepare this sandwich on smaller slices of a baguette.

2 large parisian baguettes,
ends removed, cut in half

1½ cups (355 ml) Béchamel
Sauce (recipe follows)

12 ounces (340 g) white sharp
cheddar cheese, thinly sliced

2 lb (1 kg) deli-sliced
black forest ham

3 tablespoons (45 g)
butter, melted

BÉCHAMEL SAUCE:

Makes about 2 cups

3 tablespoons (45 g)
unsalted butter

3 tablespoons (24 g) flour

1 cup (235 ml) dry white wine

1 cup (235 ml) whole milk

1 tablespoon (15 g)
Dijon mustard

¼ teaspoon (.5 g) nutmeg

salt

white pepper

[Makes 4 sandwiches]

Croque Monsieur Montréal

On a recent trip to Montreal, I was reintroduced to the Croque Monsieur, a truly gourmet ham and cheese sandwich topped with Béchamel sauce.

Preheat broiler. Slice baguettes in half horizontally. Open baguette and brush inside with melted butter. Place on a sheet pan and toast under broiler until browned, about 1 minute, then remove and set aside. On bottom half of bread, spread Béchamel sauce followed by cheddar cheese, then place under broiler to melt the cheese, about 2 minutes. Remove and top with ham and remaining cheddar cheese. Return to broiler once more to melt cheese, about 3 minutes. Remove, transfer to plate, top with top half of bread, and fold sandwich closed. Repeat process with remaining ingredients to make additional sandwiches. Serve warm with thin cut french fries.

[For béchamel sauce]
Scald the milk in a medium-sized saucepan over medium heat, stirring occasionally, until bubbles form around the sides, then turn off the heat. Melt the butter in a medium-sized skillet over medium-high heat. Add flour to butter, whisking thoroughly to combine. Cook until just turning tan in color, stirring constantly, about 3 minutes. Once roux has reached a light tan color, reduce heat to low, add the white wine, and stir vigorously to incorporate without leaving lumps. Once sauce is thick, gradually add scalded milk, ⅓ cup (75 ml) at a time, stirring vigorously and continuously between additions to prevent lumps. Add Dijon mustard and nutmeg and season with salt and pepper. The sauce is done when it coats the back of a wooden spoon. If it appears too thick, add more milk.

Inside-Out French Grilled Cheese

Turning a french baguette inside out gives you a better grilling surface for the bread.

6 (6-inch [15 cm])-long french baguettes

8 ounces (225 g) fresh buffalo mozzarella cheese, sliced thin

8 ounces (225 g) sliced provolone cheese

4 sprigs fresh tarragon, leaves removed and kept whole

2 tablespoons (28 g) butter, room temperature

Preheat panini grill to medium. Slice the baguette horizontally, taking care not to cut all the way through. Fold the baguette inside out. Top with mozzarella cheese and provolone, then sprinkle with fresh tarragon. Close baguette, butter both sides of the outside of the baguette, and place on a grill. Grill until the outsides are toasted and golden, about 3 minutes. Remove from grill or pan and let sit for about 3 minutes. Repeat process with remaining ingredients to make additional baguettes. Serve warm.

Peppered Pastrami Panini with Apples and Brie

Brie cheese is really very underrated. It's a great melting cheese, and it really adds a unique flavor to food. Paired with apples and peppered salami, Brie takes on a new life.

12 slices dark rye or pumpernickel bread

1 lb (455 g) Brie cheese

6 ounces (170 g) creamy Havarti cheese, sliced

2 Granny Smith apples, peeled, cored, and thinly sliced

6 tablespoons (90 g) butter, softened

1 lb (455 g) peppered salami, thinly sliced

3 ounces (85 g) baby spinach

Preheat panini grill. Place bread on a clean, flat, and dry work surface. Spread Brie in a thick, even layer on bread, then top with sliced apples, Havarti cheese, and the top half of sandwich. Butter both sides of sandwich and grill until browned and crisp and cheese is melted, about 10 minutes.

Remove and repeat process with remaining ingredients to make additional sandwiches.

Keep grilled sandwiches warm in 200°F (90°C) oven. Pull apart sandwiches and insert baby spinach and salami. Close, slice, and serve warm.

2 lb (1 kg) medium asparagus, ends trimmed, stalks peeled, and cut in half lengthwise

1 large Vidalia or sweet yellow onion, peeled, cut in half, and thinly sliced

3 tablespoons (45 ml) extra-virgin olive oil, plus extra for brushing

2 tablespoons (28 g) unsalted butter

2 teaspoons (5 g) grated lemon peel

¼ cup (60 ml) fresh-squeezed lemon juice

salt

coarse ground black pepper

4 fresh tarragon sprigs, stems removed and leaves chopped

12 slices crusty ciabatta bread or other crusty loaf

¼ lb (115 g) prosciutto, thinly sliced

6 ounces (170 g) Gruyere cheese, sliced

6 slices Swiss cheese

Preheat the oven to 450°F (230°C). Place the asparagus and onions on a large baking sheet, drizzle with olive oil, dot with butter, sprinkle with lemon zest and lemon juice, and season with salt and pepper. Toss the vegetables lightly to distribute the seasonings. Bake until soft and just starting to brown, about 20 minutes. Remove from oven, transfer to a bowl, toss with tarragon, then set aside.

Preheat panini grill. Place bread on a flat, clean, and dry work surface, then top with Gruyere, Swiss, and remaining slice of bread. Brush the top with olive oil and transfer to hot grill, oiled side down; brush remaining side with olive oil. Grill until cheese is melted and bread is browned and crisp, about 10 minutes.

Repeat process with remaining ingredients to make additional sandwiches.

Keep grilled sandwiches warm in a 200°F (90°C) oven. Pull sandwiches apart and insert prosciutto and asparagus and onion mixture. Close sandwiches, slice, and serve.

[Makes 6 sandwiches]

Roasted Asparagus and Sweet Onion Panini with Gruyere

Asparagus is one of my favorite vegetables, and whether it's grilled, sautéed, or roasted, it has a wonderfully unique flavor. Roasting it with onions is one way to concentrate and mix the flavors of both vegetables.

Six 4-ounce (115 g) fresh salmon fillets

olive oil

salt and coarse ground black pepper

6 french baguette rolls

1/3 cup (75 g) Lemon-Dill Mayonnaise (recipe follows)

6 leaves red leaf lettuce

2 large tomatoes, thinly sliced

12 slices smoked bacon, cooked

LEMON-DILL MAYONNAISE:

1/2 cup (112 g) good-quality mayonnaise

1 teaspoon (5 ml) fresh lemon juice

2 teaspoons (1.5 g) chopped fresh dill

salt and coarse ground black pepper

Preheat panini grill to medium-high heat. Trim salmon fillets of any fatty pieces. Rub with olive oil and season with salt and black pepper. Grill salmon for about 6 minutes, until pink and meat begins to flake. Remove from grill and set aside. Slice baguettes open lengthwise, being careful not to slice all the way through. Spread Lemon-Dill Mayonnaise on bread and top with a leaf of lettuce. Place sliced tomato on lettuce, follow with grilled salmon fillet, and finish with two slices of cooked smoked bacon. Serve.

[For the lemon-dill mayonnaise]
Combine all ingredients in a small mixing bowl. Refrigerate until ready to use.

[Makes 6 sandwiches]

Grilled Salmon and Pepper-Smoked Bacon Club

Salmon is the perfect, meaty fish for grilling. Serve warm or cool in this excellent summertime sandwich. Packing this one for a picnic is a great idea; just serve the Lemon-Dill Mayonnaise on the side.

1 zucchini, thinly sliced lengthwise

1 summer squash, thinly sliced lengthwise

2 large carrots, peeled and thickly sliced on the diagonal

¼ cup (60 ml) extra-virgin olive oil

kosher salt

coarse ground black pepper

2 avocados, peeled and thinly sliced

juice of one lemon

8 whole wheat or other flavor wraps

1 (12-ounce [340 g]) container hummus

8 leaves green or red leaf lettuce

1 english cucumber, thinly sliced on the diagonal

4 ounces (115 g) alfalfa sprouts

1 head radicchio, sliced in half and then into thin strips (optional)

8 ounces (225 g) favorite bottled ranch-style dressing

Preheat panini grill to medium-high heat. In a large bowl, toss zucchini, summer squash, and carrot slices with olive oil. Sprinkle with salt and black pepper. Leaving the grill pan open, grill the vegetables about 3 minutes per side, until tender and browned. The carrots may take a bit longer than the other vegetables, depending on the thickness of the slices. Remove vegetables from grill and set aside to cool.

Meanwhile, slice the avocado into thin strips and sprinkle with lemon juice, salt, and pepper; set aside until assembly. For assembly, lay one whole wheat wrap on a flat, clean, and dry surface. Spread hummus in an even layer on the wrap, leaving a 1 inch (2.5 cm) border around the edges of the wrap. Layer with one lettuce leaf, followed by even amounts of the grilled vegetables, cucumber, and avocado, and finishing with radicchio and alfalfa sprouts. Top the vegetables with 2 tablespoons (30 g) of ranch-style dressing. Fold the left and right sides in and over the other fold and roll the wrap. Slice wrap diagonally in half and serve.

[Makes 8 wraps]

Grilled Spring Vegetable Wrap

Top this vegetable sandwich with cool ranch dressing.

8 slices white bread

¼ cup (55 g) mayonnaise

6 leaves green lettuce, torn

12 slices peppered bacon, cooked

8 ounces (225 g) dill Havarti cheese, sliced

4 slices pumpernickel bread

¼ cup (60 g) Coleman's prepared mustard

3 plum tomatoes, thinly sliced

1½ lb (680 g) deli roast beef, sliced thin

Lay out 4 slices of white bread on a clean, dry, and flat surface. Spread each slice of bread evenly with half of the mayonnaise. Layer bread with half of the lettuce, bacon, and Havarti cheese, then top with pumpernickel bread. Spread mustard evenly over pumpernickel and top with remaining lettuce, tomato, and roast beef. Spread remaining pieces of white bread with remaining mayonnaise and place on top of sandwich, mayonnaise side down. Place a long pick or skewer in the center of all four quarters of the sandwich. Cut diagonal criss-cross cuts and serve.

[Makes 4 sandwiches]

Black and White Club

The flavor combination here is great, but the real treat is the play of colors in the layers of pumpernickel and white bread. Sliced and served in wedges, this sandwich is especially appropriate for lunchtime.

Jerked Chicken Breast Sandwich with Grilled Plantain, Sliced Mango, and Coconut Cilantro Spread

Jerked chicken is an easy way to pack a punch into any sandwich. Choose from numerous jerked seasonings available in the spice aisle or marinade section of your local supermarket, or use your own time-tested favorite. Don't be afraid to spice it up—the Coconut Cilantro Spread will cool it down.

4 (4-ounce [115 g]) boneless, skinless chicken breasts

3 tablespoons (45 ml) olive oil

1/4 cup (60 g) Jamaican jerk seasoning

1 tablespoon (20 g) honey

2 ripe plantains

1 mango, peeled, cored, and thinly sliced

8 slices large peasant bread

1/3 cup (75 ml) Coconut Cilantro Spread (recipe follows)

COCONUT CILANTRO SPREAD:

Makes about 1/2 cup (120 ml)

1/4 cup (60 ml) Thai coconut sauce

1/4 cup (16 g) fresh cilantro leaves, coarsely chopped

2 tablespoons (30 ml) lime juice

Place chicken in a bowl and add olive oil, jerk seasoning, and honey. Marinate for at least 1 hour. Peel plantains and cut into 1/4-inch (0.6 cm) -thick slices on the diagonal. Coat slices with olive oil and set aside. Preheat panini grill to high, then reduce heat to medium-high. Grill chicken until cooked through, about 7 minutes. Remove and let cool for about 5 minutes. Slice thinly, cutting with the grain of the meat. Grill plantain slices until golden and tender, about 3 minutes per side. Lay out bread slices and spread evenly with Coconut Cilantro Spread, then layer chicken, plantains, and mango. Add second slice of bread, slice in half, and serve.

[For coconut cilantro spread]
Combine all ingredients in a small mixing bowl, cover, and refrigerate for at least 30 minutes.

6 (8-ounce [225 g]) boneless, skinless chicken breasts

1½ cups (355 ml) barbecue sauce

1 tablespoon (15 ml) liquid smoke

1 tablespoon (15 ml) Worcestershire sauce

1 tablespoon (20 g) honey

1 tablespoon (10 g) minced fresh garlic

1 tablespoon (6 g) coarse ground black pepper

6 ounces (170 g) smoked Gouda or mozzarella cheese, thinly sliced

1 large red onion, thinly sliced

½ cup (20 g) loosely packed cilantro leaves

6 ciabatta rolls, horizontally sliced

Combine barbecue sauce, liquid smoke, Worcestershire sauce, honey, garlic, and pepper in a large bowl. Set aside half of the sauce mixture. Add chicken to original bowl of sauce mixture, toss to coat, then cover and marinate for at least 30 minutes. Preheat panini grill to high. Grill chicken until tender and cooked through, about 7 minutes. Remove from grill and set aside. Thinly coat the onions with olive oil and sprinkle with black pepper. Grill on high heat until tender, about 4 minutes on each side. Remove from heat and let cool.

Once chicken is cool enough to handle, pull strips of chicken apart or slice thin and toss in ¼ cup (60 ml) of reserved barbecue sauce. Lay out bottoms of rolls, coat with a thin layer of barbecue sauce. Dividing ingredients evenly among sandwiches, top with cilantro leaves, red onions, chicken, and cheese. Brush inside of top half of rolls with remaining barbecue sauce and top sandwichs. Serve.

[Makes 6 sandwiches]

Barbecue Chicken and Gouda on Ciabatta

Ciabatta bread is the quintessential "panini" bread, yielding beautifully grilled sandwiches. Here, smoked Gouda pairs with hearty barbecued chicken to make a perfect summer treat.

1 medium red pepper

1 medium yellow pepper

1 medium orange pepper

$\frac{1}{2}$ cup (120 ml) extra-virgin olive oil, plus extra for brushing peppers

1$\frac{1}{2}$ teaspoons (7.5 g) Dijon mustard

1 tablespoon (15 ml) balsamic vinegar

1 tablespoon (4 g) chopped fresh parsley

1 tablespoon (3 g) minced sun-dried tomato

1 teaspoon (4 g) minced fresh garlic

1 teaspoon (6 g) kosher salt

coarse ground black pepper

1 (9" [23 cm]) round loaf focaccia

$\frac{1}{3}$ cup (75 g) prepared black olive paste

4 ounces (115 g) goat cheese, crumbled

$\frac{1}{2}$ medium red onion, thinly sliced (optional)

6 ounces (170 g) marinated artichoke hearts

6 ounces (170 g) prosciutto, thinly sliced

6 ounces (170 g) peppered salami, thinly sliced

4 ounces (115 g) pepperoni, thinly sliced

8 ounces (225 g) fresh buffalo mozzarella cheese, thinly sliced

½ cup (20 g) loosely packed fresh basil leaves

Preheat panini to high. Rub peppers with olive oil, then place on hot grill and cook until charred, 8 to 10 minutes. Remove from heat and place in a brown paper bag. Seal bag by rolling top and set aside for 5 to 10 minutes. Remove from bag and use fingers to rub charred skin away from flesh. Remove seeds and stems, then slice peppers into 1-inch (2.5 cm) strips and set aside.

Combine mustard, balsamic vinegar, parsley, sun-dried tomato, and garlic in the bowl of a food processor fitted with the blade attachment, and pulse until pureed. With the processor running slowly, add ½ cup (120 ml) olive oil in a steady stream to emulsify. Transfer to bowl, season with salt and pepper, cover, and refrigerate.

Slice focaccia in half horizontally. Remove top and set aside. Drizzle bottom of focaccia with one-third of the vinaigrette, then layer with an even coat of olive paste followed by roasted peppers, goat cheese, red onion, and artichoke hearts. Arrange the mozzarella cheese over the artichoke hearts and layer with prosciutto, salami, and pepperoni. Drizzle with one-third of the vinaigrette and top with basil and chives. Drizzle inside of top half of focaccia with remaining vinaigrette. Place on sandwich, vinaigrette side down.

Wrap sandwich in parchment paper and refrigerate for at least 1 hour before serving. If making sandwich in advance, reserve vinaigrette for dipping or drizzle the insides of the top and bottom of the focaccia just before serving.

[Serves 6 to 8]

Antipasto-Stuffed Focaccia Party Sandwich

This one is big enough to invite the friends over. For the peppers, you can substitute any combination of three colored peppers except green.

2 japanese eggplants, peeled and sliced ½" (1.3 cm) thick

olive oil for grilling

6 large syrian (pita) breads

1 lb (455 g) shaved roasted leg of lamb or deli roast beef, thinly sliced

8 ounces (225 g) feta cheese, crumbled

½ cup (16 g) loosely packed italian flat leaf parsley

2 small vine-ripened tomatoes, sliced thin

1 cup (235 ml) Tzatziki Sauce (recipe follows)

TZATZIKI SAUCE:

Makes about 1 cup (235 ml)

½ cup (50 g) peeled, seeded, and finely chopped cucumber

½ cup (120 ml) plain yogurt

1 teaspoon (5 ml) olive oil

1 teaspoon (5 ml) lemon juice

¼ teaspoon (1.5 g) kosher salt

½ teaspoon (.5 g) chopped fresh oregano

1 teaspoon (3 g) minced fresh garlic

1 teaspoon (.3 g) minced fresh dill (optional)

Preheat panini grill to high heat. Rub eggplant slices with olive oil and sprinkle with pepper. Grill until golden, about 4 minutes per side. Remove from heat and set aside to cool. Place eggplant slices on one half of pita bread. Top with parsley, shaved lamb or roast beef, feta cheese, and tomatoes. Drizzle with Tzatziki Sauce and fold pita over. Repeat process with remaining ingredients to make additional pitas. Serve.

[For tzatziki sauce]
Combine all ingredients in a bowl, cover, and refrigerate for at least 1 hour.

[Makes 6 wraps]

Folded Greek Syrian with Traditional Tzatziki Sauce

Tzatziki sauce is a traditional Greek complement to lamb sandwiches. I borrowed this wonderful recipe from Emeril Lagasse.

1 large loaf rosemary focaccia, or 6 rolls

¼ cup (55 g) Pesto Mayonnaise (recipe follows)

1 cup (60 g) mixed field greens

2 vine-ripened tomatoes, thinly sliced

6 ounces (170 g) fresh mozzarella, thinly sliced

⅓ cup (75 ml) balsamic vinaigrette salad dressing

4 (8-ounce [227 g]) boneless, skinless chicken breasts, grilled and thinly sliced

1 medium red onion, thinly sliced

PESTO MAYONNAISE:

Makes about ⅓ cup (75 g)

⅓ cup (75 g) mayonnaise

1 tablespoon (14 g) sour cream

3 tablespoons (45 ml) favorite basil pesto

½ teaspoon (1 g) coarse ground black pepper

[Serves 6]

Tuscan Chicken on Rosemary Focaccia

When I think of Tuscany, I imagine beautiful, lush countryside, perfect for a spontaneous picnic. This sandwich is best enjoyed with perfectly ripened tomatoes.

Slice open the focaccia loaf horizontally, then generously coat inside of both sides with pesto mayonnaise. Layer bottom half with lettuce, red onion, mozzarella, tomato, and chicken. Drizzle with balsamic vinaigrette and close with top half of roll. Repeat process with remaining ingredients to make additional sandwiches. Serve.

[For pesto mayonnaise]
Combine all ingredients in mixing bowl and stir. Cover and refrigerate for at least 30 minutes.

Index

About the Author

Dwayne Ridgaway, although a native of Kerrville, Texas, now lives in Bristol, Rhode Island. He is the author of Lasagna: **The Art of Layered Cooking** and **Pizza: 50 Traditional and Alternative Recipes for the Oven and Grill**, and a contributing writer, food stylist, and recipe developer for several cooking magazines. Dwayne currently works in Rhode Island as a food and beverage consultant, caterer, and event designer. A graduate of the highly respected Johnson and Wales University, Dwayne has made a career out of exploring and celebrating the culinary arts. His passions lie in fresh ingredients and new flavors. Exploring everything the world has to offer in both techniques and flavors, Dwayne makes it his goal to combine these elements with inspired cooking to develop recipes that anyone can execute and enjoy. With **Sandwiches, Panini, and Wraps**, Dwayne hopes home cooks everywhere will begin to explore their tastes and passions and use his recipes and writing as groundwork for their own personal creativity.

Panini and Other Great Grilled Sandwiches